AF151837

YOUR KNOWLEDGE HAS VALUE

- We will publish your bachelor's and master's thesis, essays and papers

- Your own eBook and book - sold worldwide in all relevant shops

- Earn money with each sale

Upload your text at www.GRIN.com and publish for free

Alikira Richard

Ontology the novice perspective

Understanding Ontology

GRIN Publishing

Bibliographic information published by the German National Library:

The German National Library lists this publication in the National Bibliography; detailed bibliographic data are available on the Internet at http://dnb.dnb.de .

Imprint:

Copyright © 2012 GRIN Verlag GmbH
Print and binding: Books on Demand GmbH, Norderstedt Germany
ISBN: 978-3-656-33668-6

This book at GRIN:

http://www.grin.com/en/e-book/206341/ontology-the-novice-perspective

GRIN - Your knowledge has value

Since its foundation in 1998, GRIN has specialized in publishing academic texts by students, college teachers and other academics as e-book and printed book. The website www.grin.com is an ideal platform for presenting term papers, final papers, scientific essays, dissertations and specialist books.

Visit us on the internet:

http://www.grin.com/

http://www.facebook.com/grincom

http://www.twitter.com/grin_com

A paper presented by Alikira Richard as an assignment for the completion of coursework on philosophy of computing and information technology

ONTOLOGY

Overview

Ontology has been attracting a lot of attention recently. While ontology research begun in the early 90's in the knowledge base community, the research activity has been accelerated and spread over the web technology community by the semantic web movement in the last few years. Many people talk about ontology nowadays. However, there seems to be some misunderstandings about what ontology is and what ontological engineering is, how it is useful, etc. The purpose of this tutorial is to clarify issues on ontology and ontological engineering and to describe the author's personal views on how ontological engineering should contribute to the future knowledge processing.

What Is Ontology?

In a lay man's term, ontology is the theory of being as such. It was originally called "first philosophy" by Aristotle. In the 18th century Christian Wolff contrasted ontology, or general metaphysics, with special metaphysical theories of souls, bodies, or God, claiming that ontology could be a deductive discipline revealing the essences of things. This view was later strongly criticized by David Hume and Immanuel Kant. Ontology was revived in the early 20th century by practitioners of phenomenology and existentialism, notably Edmund Husserl and his student Heidegger. The American heritage dictionary defines Ontology as a philosophical inquiry into the nature of being itself, a branch of metaphysics. While Aristotle defined ontology as the science of being as such. The science of being is used in many different senses. It is sometimes considered to be identical to metaphysics, but preferably used in a more specific sense, as that part of metaphysics that specifies the most fundamental categories of existence and elementary substances or structures out of which the world is made.

Of late, the field of ontology has become a popular technique in Artificial Intelligence. It is used to define the building blocks out of which models of the world are made. Hence it is referred to as the basic level of a knowledge representation.

Ontology deals with the nature and the organization of reality and it tries to answer questions like "what is existence?", "what properties can explain existence?", among others. Unlike the special sciences, each of which investigates a class of beings and their determinations, ontology regards all the species as qua being and the attributes that belong to it qua being.

Ontology is a formal, explicit specification of a shared conceptualization. Whereby a "conceptualization" is an abstract model of a phenomenon, created by identification of the relevant concepts of the phenomenon. The concepts, the relations between them and the constraints on their use are explicitly defined. "Formal" means that Ontology is machine-readable and excludes the use of natural languages. For example, in medical domains, the concepts are diseases and symptoms, the relations between them are causal and a constraint is that a disease cannot cause itself. Ontology is a "shared conceptualization" states that Ontologies aim to represent consensual knowledge intended for the use of a group. Ideally the Ontology captures knowledge independently of its use and in a way that can be shared universally, but practically different tasks and uses call for different representations of the knowledge in Ontology

Definitions

There are many interpretations about what ontology is. In fact, hot discussions are often done in many meetings on ontology.

1) In philosophy, it means theory of existence. It tries to explain what is being and how the world is configured by introducing a system of critical categories to account things and their intrinsic relations.

2) From AI point of view, ontology is defined as "explicit specification of conceptualization".

3) From a knowledge-based systems point of view, it is defined as "a theory (system) of concepts/ vocabulary used as building blocks of an information processing system" (Mizoguchi, 1995). In a context of problem solving, ontologies are divided into two types: Task ontology for problem solving process and domain ontology for the domain where the task is performed.

4) Gruber] defines ontology as an agreement about shared conceptualizations where shared conceptualizations include conceptual frameworks for modeling domain knowledge; content-specific protocols for communication among inter-operating agents; and agreements about the representation of particular domain theories.

In the knowledge sharing context, ontologies are specified in the form of definitions of representational vocabulary. A very simple case would be a type hierarchy, specifying classes and their sub-assumption relationships. Relational database schemas also serve as ontologies by specifying the relations that can exist in some shared database and the integrity constraints that must hold for them.

Thus an ontology consists of concepts, hierarchical (is-a) organization of them, relations among them (in addition to is-a and part-of), axioms to formalize the definitions and relations.

Why Study Ontology?

In recent years the development of ontologies explicit formal specification of the terms in the domain and relations among them (Gruber, 1993) has been moving from the realm of

2

Artificial-Intelligence laboratories to the desktops of domain experts, and they have become common on the World-Wide Web.

The ontologies on the Web range from large taxonomies categorizing Web sites (such as on Yahoo!) to categorizations of products for sale and their features such as on Amazon.com. According to Brickley and Guha (1999), the WWW Consortium (W3C) is developing the Resource Description Framework, a language for encoding knowledge on Web pages to make it understandable to electronic agents searching for information.
The Defense Advanced Research Projects Agency (DARPA), in conjunction with the W3C, is developing DARPA Agent Markup Language (DAML) by extending RDF with more expressive constructs aimed at facilitating agent interaction on the Web. Many disciplines now develop standardized ontologies that domain experts can use to share and annotate information in their fields. Medicine, for example, has produced large, standardized, structured vocabularies such as SNOMED (Price and Spackman 2000) and the semantic network of the Unified Medical Language System (Humphreys and Lindberg 1993). Broad general-purpose ontologies are emerging as well.

For example, the United Nations Development Program and Dun & Bradstreet combined their efforts to develop the UNSPSC ontology which provides terminology for products and services.

Lastly, Ontology defines a common vocabulary for researchers who need to share information in a domain. It includes machine-interpretable definitions of basic concepts in the domain and relations among them. Reasons as to why someone may want to develop ontology include the following: To share common understanding of the structure of information among people or software agents, To enable reuse of domain knowledge, To make domain assumptions explicit, To separate domain knowledge from the operational knowledge, and To analyze domain knowledge.

Sharing common understanding of the structure of information among people or software agents is one of the more common goals in developing ontologies (Gruber 1993). For example, suppose several different Web sites contain medical information or provide medical e-commerce services. If these Web sites share and publish the same underlying ontology of the terms they all use, then computer agents can extract and aggregate information from these different sites. The agents can use this aggregated information to answer user queries or as input data to other applications.

Enabling reuse of domain knowledge is one of the driving forces behind recent surge in ontology research. For example, models for many different domains need to represent the notion of time. This representation includes the notions of time intervals, points in time, relative measures of time, and so on. If one group of researchers develops such ontology in detail, others can simply reuse it for their domains. Additionally, if we need to build a large ontology, we can integrate several existing ontologies describing portions of the large domain. We can also reuse a general ontology, such as the UNSPSC ontology, and extend it to describe our domain of interest.

Making explicit domain assumptions underlying implementation makes it possible to change these assumptions easily in the event that our knowledge about the domain changes. Hard-coding assumptions about the world in programming-language code make these assumptions not only hard to find and understand but also hard to change, in particular for someone without programming expertise. In addition, explicit specifications of domain knowledge are useful for new users who must learn what terms in the domain mean.

Separating the domain knowledge from the operational knowledge is another common use of ontologies. We can describe a task of configuring a product from its components according to a required specification and implement a program that does this configuration independent of the products and components themselves. We can then develop ontology of PC-components and characteristics and apply the algorithm to configure made-to-order PCs. We can also use the same algorithm to configure elevators if we feed elevator component ontology to it .

Analyzing domain knowledge is possible once a declarative specification of the terms is available. Formal analysis of terms is extremely valuable when both attempting to reuse existing ontologies and extending them.

Often ontology of the domain is not a goal in itself. Developing ontology is akin to defining a set of data and their structure for other programs to use. Problem-solving methods, domain-independent applications, and software agents use ontologies and knowledge bases built from ontologies as data. For example, in this paper we develop ontology of wine and food and appropriate combinations of wine with meals. This ontology can then be used as a basis for some applications in a suite of restaurant-managing tools: One application could create wine suggestions for the menu of the day or answer queries of waiters and customers. Another application could analyze an inventory list of a wine cellar and suggest which wine categories to expand and which particular wines to purchase for upcoming menus or cookbooks.

Types of Ontology
There are a few types of ontologies which have different roles. In some cases, discussion goes to a mess because of the ignorance of what type of ontology is under consideration. Some say "ontology is domain-specific like a knowledge base which was a failure". Others say "No, it isn't". Ontology is very generic and hence it is widely applicable and sharable. Both are correct because there are several types of ontology which have been discussed below.

Upper Ontology
Philosophers have tackled what is being for about two thousand years. The portion of their work includes higher level categories which explain what exist in the world, which is called upper ontology.

Task ontology and Domain ontology

Task ontology is useful for describing inherent problem solving structure of the existing tasks domain-independently. It is obtained by analyzing task structures of real world problems. It does not cover the control structure but do components or primitives of unit inferences taking place during performing tasks. The ultimate goal of task ontology research includes providing a theory of all the vocabulary/concepts necessary for building a model of human problem solving processes. The determination of the abstraction level of task ontology requires a close consideration on granularity and generality of the unit of problem solving action. These observations suggest task ontology consists of the following four kinds of concepts.

1) Task roles reflecting the roles played by the domain objects in the problem solving process
2) Task actions representing unit activities appearing in the problem solving process,
3) States of the objects, and
4) Other concepts specific to the task.

Task ontology for a scheduling task, for example, includes:

1) Task roles: Scheduling recipient, Scheduling resource, Due date, Schedule, Constraints, Goal, Priority, etc.
2) Task actions: Assign, Classify, Pick up, Select Relax, Neglect, etc.
3) States: Unassigned, The last, Idle etc.

Actions are defined as a set of procedures representing its operational meaning. So, they collectively serve as a set of reusable components for building a scheduling engine. Task ontology thus helps develop use-neutral domain ontology.

Heavy-weight ontology and light-weight ontology

Another viewpoint suggests Light-weight ontology and heavy-weight ontology. The former includes ontologies for web search engines like Yahoo ontology which consists of a topic hierarchy with little consideration of rigorous definition of a concept, principle of concept organization, distinction between word and concept, etc. The main purpose of such a hierarchy is to power up the search engine and hence it is very use-dependent. The latter is different. It includes ontologies developed with much attention paid to rigorous meaning of each concept, organizing principles developed in philosophy, semantically rigorous relations between concepts, etc. Instance models are usually built based on those ontologies to model a target world, which requires careful conceptualization of the world to guarantee of the consistency and fidelity of the model. Upper ontology is a typical ontology of heavy-weight ontology.

Ontology is not just a set of terms .While ontology provides us with a common vocabulary, a vocabulary, which is a set of terms, itself cannot be said to be an ontology as it is. An ontology needs to consists of is-a hierarchy of concepts. This is partly because it reveals the proper classification of concepts to show inherent structure of the target world. Furthermore, there should be a clear distinction between term/word and concepts. The former are names of the latter and ontology is a theory of concepts rather than terms/word. It does not care about how the concept is called. It puts an appropriate name on a concept for making it human understandable. This suggests the synonym is not an ontological issue.

Roles of ontology

The following is an enumeration of the merits we can enjoy from ontology:

A common vocabulary; the description of the target world needs a vocabulary agreed by people involved. The fundamental role of ontology is to provide a common vocabulary.

Data structure; ontology in a database is the conceptual schema. In this sense, ontology provides us with a data structure appropriate for information description and exchange.

Explanation of what is left implicit; In all of the human activities, we find presuppositions/assumptions which are left implicit. Typical examples include definitions of common and basic terms, relations and constraints among them, and viewpoints for interpreting the phenomena and target structure common to the tasks they are usually engaged in. Any knowledge base built is based on a conceptualization possessed by the builder and is usually implicit. Ontology is an explication of such implicit knowledge. An explicit representation of such assumptions and conceptualization is more than a simple explication. Although it might be hard to be properly appreciated by people who have no experience in such representation, its contribution to knowledge reuse and sharing is more than expectation considering that the implicitness has been one of the crucial causes of preventing knowledge sharing and reuse.

Semantic interoperability; Metadata used in semantic web is built on the basis of ontology which constrains and partially defines the meaning of each tags and values. Interpretation and translation of the metadata can be done via ontologies. Ontologies thus play the role of glue which guarantees semantic interoperability among metadata.

Explication of design rationale; ontology contributes to explication of assumptions, implicit preconditions required by the problems to solve as well as the conceptualization of the target object which reflects those assumptions. In diagnostic systems, for instance, fault classes diagnosed and range of the diagnostic inference are typical examples.

Systematization of knowledge; Knowledge systematization requires well-established vocabulary/concepts in terms of which people describe phenomena, theories and target things under consideration. Ontology thus contributes to providing backbone of systematization of knowledge.

Meta-model function; A model is usually built in the computer as an abstraction of the real-world target. And, ontology provides us with concepts and relations among them which are used as building blocks of the model. Thus, ontology specifies the models to build by giving guidelines and constraints which should be satisfied.

Theory of content; In summary, an ontology provides us with "a theory of content" to enable research results to accumulate like form-oriented research avoiding ad-hoc methodologies which the conventional content-centered activities have been suffering from.

Ontological engineering

For ontological art to become a reality a form system development life cycle must be established or adopted. The traditional phases of SDLC can be used sequentially. These phases are:

Analysis phase
A requirements specification document should be prepared and it must contain The purpose of the ontology, level of the formality of the ontology , boundaries of (Scope) and a description of key terms to be used

Knowledge Acquisition phase during this phase
Knowledge from respective domains is captured. This can be done through interviews with expert and then presenting expert views in a programming language.

Conceptualization
Here a glossary of terms to be used and their definitions is created and categorized accordingly.

Integration phase
To reuse definitions in other ontologies, Inspect meta-ontologies to select those that best fit the conceptualization from other ontologies and reuse them.

Implementation phase
The ontology is codified in a formal ontology language.

Evaluation
Verify the correctness of the ontology and validate that the ontology represents the System it is supposed

Documentation phase
Each phase of the development life cycle is documented. The different documentations from different phases are put together to form what is known as system documentation.

Booch, G., Rumbaugh, J. and Jacobson, I. (1997).*The Unified Modeling Language user guide*: Addison-Wesley.

Breuker, J. and de Velde, W., V. (1994) The Common KADS Library for Expertise Modeling, *IOS Press*, Amsterdam.

Chandrasekaran, B. (1986). Generic tasks in knowledge-based reasoning: High-level building blocks for expert system design, *IEEE Expert*, (1), No.3.

Genesereth, M. & Nilsson, N. (1987) *Foundation of Artificial Intelligence*.

Gruber, T. http://www-ksl.stanford.edu/kst/ what-is-an-ontology.html.

Guarino N. (1997), Some Organizing Principles for a Unified Top-Level Ontology. Revised version of a paper appeared at *AAAI 1997 Spring Symposium on Ontological Engineering* (LADSEB-CNR Int. Rep. 02/97)

Guarino, N. (1998). Some Ontological Principles for Designing Upper Level Lexical Resources. *Proc. of the First International Conference on Lexical Resources and studies of knowledge engineering Proc. of 5th IJCAI.*

Uschold, M. & Gruninger, M. (1996). Ontologies: Principles, Methods and Applications. *Knowledge Engineering Review* 11 (2).

www.unspsc.org